Glycerin Soap Making

Beginners Guide to 26 Easy "Melt and Pour Method" Glycerin Soap Recipes Using Only Natural Organic Ingredients

Copyright © 2016 Rose Michaels

All Rights Reserved.

DISCLAIMER

All rights reserved. No part of this publication or the information in it may be quoted from or reproduced in any form by means such as printing, scanning, photocopying or otherwise without prior written permission of the copyright holder.

Effort has been made to ensure that the information in this book is accurate and complete, however, the author and the publisher do not warrant the accuracy of the information, text and graphics contained within the book due to the rapidly changing nature of science, research, known and unknown facts and internet. The Author and the publisher do not hold any responsibility for errors, omissions or contrary interpretation of the subject matter herein. This book is presented solely for motivational and informational purposes only.

Table of Contents

Introduction 5

There are Many Reasons to Make Your Own Soap 9

The Essentials You Need to Make Glycerin Soap 13

The Basic Tools that You Need for Making Glycerin Soap 15

Tips and Techniques for a Successful Process 18

A Few Precautions to Consider 23

The Ultimate Glycerin Soap Recipes Collection 25

The Mint Connection 29
    Mint Mania 30
    Mint and Lavender Tranquility Bar 32
    Chocolate and Mint Divine 34
    Mint Love 36

Rolling with the Rosemary 39
    The Rosemary Rage 40
    Rosemary and Lavender Love 41
    It's Thyme for Rosemary Glycerin Soap Bar 43
    Rugged Rosemary Renegade 45

Fruity-Tooty and Fabulous 47
    Orange You Going to X-presso Yourself! 48
    Strawberry Heaven 50

Lemon Lime Divine 52
　　The Facial Fruit Smoothie 54

Tea Glee 55
　　Roses and Tea Bar 56
　　Chamomile Comfort 58
　　The Tea Tree Experience 60
　　Tea Time 2 Bath Time 62

Oatmeal Obsessions 65
　　Oatmeal and Blueberry Bar 66
　　Oatmeal, Honey, and Vanilla Beauty Blast Bar 68
　　Peach and Oatmeal Exfoliating Bar 70
　　The Avocado Oatmeal Adventure 72

Divinely Different—In a World all their Own
.. 73
　　Ah, What a Relief Bar! 74
　　Chocolate and Cinnamon Swirl Bar 76
　　Aloe Vera Gel and Cucumber Peel Rejuvenator
　　.. 78
　　Sunshine in a Bar 80
　　The Fiesta 82
　　Flower Power Bar 84

Conclusion 86

Introduction

We all know why we us soap. It's important to be clean and sanitary so we avoid health risks and just simply feel better. What feels better than feeling clean? However, all soaps are not created equal and that is where the problem lies. This book, will help you gain a better understanding of all things glycerin soap related. And we believe you'll be excited and want to give it a try. Why? We've taken away all the worries and given you a step-by-step plan that will help you to:

- Begin using natural soaps instead of chemically processed bar soaps
- Save money
- Bring some aromatherapy into your life that can literally be used
- Learn a skill that is as good to know as it is healthy
- With each chapter, you'll be a step closer to gaining a full understanding of the ways that making organic glycerin soap can happen in your life—regardless of how busy you are or how much or little you know at this very minute. We've got you covered!
- Learn about all the reasons that you would want to invest in the time and resources to make your own soap.

- Discover what the necessary ingredients and tools are that you need to make nearly any type of glycerin soap that you may want to.
- We'll share some tips and techniques with you that help you have success in your soap making adventures.
- Take some time to review the few precautions you may want to consider. Glycerin soap is healthy, but as with all things, there are some things that you should be aware of when you begin the process.
- Then, finally, you're going to get to dive into the most exciting part of the book, the part you've been waiting for—the recipes. These are fantastic recipes, proven and tested by those glycerin soap aficionados that have made this such a popular activity. The types of

soaps we will share recipes for mostly work for your entire family and they include:

- Mint-based soaps
- Rosemary-based soaps
- Glycerin soaps with fruit in them
- Tea-based soaps
- Oatmeal infused bars
- Some glycerin soap recipes that just can't be put into any category at all

Hopefully you're excited and ready to get going! We've put a lot of love and care into creating this book for you, because we believe in organic glycerin soap. It's good for you and what's good for you is always something worth focusing your time and attention on!

There are Many Reasons to Make Your Own Soap

There are times when you likely think, oh no, I just don't think I have time to take on one more thing. Maybe some 'other time' when I have more free time. This is a logical thought, of course, and one that most people can sympathize with. We are busy and lives are chaotic enough without adding something else to the plate. However...

What if adding something else to the plate—making your own glycerin soap in this case—ended up revealing that it was a simple, surprising way to make your life better in some way? Actually, in many ways! You'd likely give it a try if you know that. We've put together some interesting feedback from those who have been where you are today, not sure if they wanted to invest their time and resources in creating glycerin soap. Maybe one or two of these points will resonate with you. It's more likely that they will all have appeal, because they make sense.

1. When you create your own soaps you have complete control of every ingredient that goes into the bar you're making. That means there are no chemicals, because no one will put chemicals into a product that touches their skin, intentionally.
2. Through the process of selecting the ingredients you want in your soap, you can pick and choose those perfect blend of scents and additions to your soap that appeal to you. Think about it...have you ever looked at a product that seemed interesting and thought, I wish they had this scent?
3. Homemade glycerin soaps make excellent gift ideas for the holidays and even little party favors if you are ever the hostess for an event. Some of the cleverest ideas that we've heard of include: bridal shower gifts (with the bride-

to-be's favorite aromas), gift basket additions, and donations to fundraising for schools or organizations.

4. The more we can do for ourselves in our lives, particularly with products that we need, the better able we are to control our finances. We can budget better, too.

5. These types of projects are wonderful ways to take a break from other areas of life that may be stressful or taxing. While getting that reprieve, we can bring out our creativity. Trying something new is always great for us because it motivates us and often inspires, as well.

6. If you have specific needs that you want to focus on, dry skin or sensitive skin for example, you can do minimal research and invest a little time in making the soap and end

up with a product that works phenomenally well for you.

7. Get creative and try making things like soap on a rope, different colored soaps, and little unique soap collections that are just as much décor as they are function.

These are seven great reasons as to why you should consider making your own glycerin soap. Perhaps with a little thought or awareness about your own life and specific personal needs, you might come up with a reason we didn't even list. Either way, we're set to move to the next chapter. It's time to learn about the essentials that you need to begin the creative process. Through this process you will begin taking control of the soap that you use on your skin and consequently, what products your loved ones are using on theirs.

The Essentials You Need to Make Glycerin Soap

With a few basic ingredients and tools as your starting point, you will have all the basics that you need to begin making glycerin soap that is all natural and absolutely awesome! The only "extras" you will need to seek out are the ones that make the soap blend that you want (your ingredients that customize the bar).

The Base Ingredients for Making Most Glycerin Soaps

These ingredients are easy to find at most natural products stores, online retailers, craft stores, and even at department stores—which are increasing the amount of natural and organic products they offer. Your only rule to be concerned about is that you are using organic products with good reputations (which you can find from reviews).

- Melt and pour soap: this is also known as glycerin soap.
- Rubbing alcohol: this is used for helping to set some soaps, but you'll want to make sure that you're not sensitive to it, and will not want to use it for clear soaps (as it can sometimes turn them cloudy).

The Basic Tools that You Need for Making Glycerin Soap

Many of these tools are going to be things that your kitchen is already equipped with and it is okay to use the same tools that you'd use to cook your food. After all, these are all natural ingredients that cannot harm you.

- Measuring spoons and cups: using the right amount of ingredients is important to how the glycerin soap will turn out. If you have stainless steel cups and spoons - they work the best, as they are durable and easy to clean.

- Food scale: kitchen scales for food are a wonderful way to weigh out ingredients.

- A double boiler: non-stick cookware is fantastic!

- A metal whisk: easy to clean and a wonderful way to mix your ingredients together in your soap mixture.

- Spatula: just like with anything you mix for baking, glycerin soap will stick to the sides of the bowls and you want to use as much of it as you can!

- Cutting board: most types of boards are great, but you are best off not using a wooden cutting board, as it will likely be a messier clean-up.

- Large knife: a large, sharpened chef's knife is excellent for cutting your soap if you dry it in a solid block and then cut into squares (in lieu of a mold).

- Spray bottle: this is for the rubbing alcohol. Make sure you mark it!

- Soap mold(s): with the soap molds is where you can really have fun and go wild. They have shapes, squares, circles, and they all come in various sizes. When starting out, you may want to go for the basic square mold until you get the hang of it. However, if you're feeling like a "let's go crazy" glycerin soap maker, go with whatever strikes your fancy. Just Google glycerin soap molds to find more options than you may ever have thought possible.

You've got the basic ingredients down. You've got your tools ready. What comes next is understanding the tips and techniques that will lead to your success when you start creating.

Tips and Techniques for a Successful Process

It's easy to have success in your glycerin soap making endeavors. And better yet—you can have it by learning from the mistakes that others have made. These little "tricks of the trade" that we've compiled for you come from people who've been making glycerin soaps for years. By keep them in mind, you will save yourself time and money, as well.

1. Grease your molds before you start to make the soap. This will prevent the soap from

setting before you even get it into the molds. Smart thinking, right?

2. Take a few extra minutes to measure out your ingredients before you start combining them. This will allow you to move more quickly once you start and not feel pressured as you try to mix this while measuring that. Remember, it's supposed to be fun to make these soaps!

3. Consider using sunflower oil instead of water to mix any powdered pigments that you may want to work with. This will prevent clumping, which is very bothersome if you tend to teeter on the brink of perfectionism.

4. If you find that you have an affinity and love for soap making, you'll want to begin purchasing your main ingredients in bulk to save you some money. They have a long shelf

life so you don't have to worry about anything going bad.

5. Explore different scents and find the essential oils that you like best and will use most so they are handy. They make all the difference, really, and even allow you the option of using the soap as a decorative, wonderfully scented accent piece.

6. If you have honey as a part of your recipe, making sure you warm it up a bit before mixing it in with the soap. This will make it a lot easier during the blending process. NOTE: don't warm it up so much that it gets harder and too thick, though, because that will not make things easier at all. You can put the honey container into a bowl of warm water to do this—it works great. Worst case scenario, make sure the honey is at room temperature!

7. Some people like a cutting board just for their soap because they can draw lines on it so they know exactly where to cut their soap when it is complete. It's a great idea, and for something like this, they often recommend going to a garage sale or thrift store to purchase the board you'll use. It doesn't have to be brand new to be awesome! And remember—avoid wood cutting boards if you can. This is an option if you don't want to invest in soap molds right away.

8. Don't clean your soap making equipment right away when you are done. This may seem completely wrong, but when you clean things immediately, you're likely to have a greasy mess that is more frustrating and time consuming than it would have to be if you just waited. Go ahead...wait...you can do it!

9. Silicon molds are typically the easiest to work with.

10. Be patient when stirring your soap mixture and go slowly so ingredients don't sploosh and splash everywhere. AND...stir by hand.

11. If you are doing the sniff test for your soap to make sure it's perfect, make sure you smell some coffee grounds first, because they will help neutralize your nose and you'll be able to embrace the true aroma coming from your soap.

Eleven fantastic tips to help you make the most of your glycerin soap making adventures. You don't have to have years of experience to create soap like a pro from day one.

A Few Precautions to Consider

Since you are working with organic, natural ingredients to make soaps the risks are minimal, but it is always important to know your body and what it may negatively respond to, as well as the same information for the people that may be using the soap that you make.

Consider what you may be allergic to. Most people are not allergic to natural ingredients, but on occasion, you'll find someone who is, particularly with fruits. Other ingredients such as lye and rubbing alcohol may create problems for some individuals, even if they are natural. Just be aware. A clever and effective solution to this is to create little ingredient labels for the soap you make if you are going to give it as a gift. Then others know and you can have peace of mind.

You'll also want to make sure that the tools you use that are washable, such as clothes and coverings for the soap are washed in a separate load and not with your other laundry. It's a great idea in case there is coloring, lye, or some other ingredient that maybe shouldn't be mixed with the rest of your laundry. It's always better to be safe than sorry!

The last thing you will want to pay attention to are the curious little minds and people that may be around you. Young children love to experiment and are often curious about what you are doing in the kitchen. Set the ground rules and find a few ways in which they can participate if you want, otherwise, you may want to save your glycerin soap making projects for after their sweet little selves are down to sleep for the night.

The Ultimate Glycerin Soap Recipes Collection

Let's start off by giving you a basic overview of the process for creating most recipes. After that, we'll share 26 recipes with you that are likely to make it hard to choose which one to begin with. Our recommendation—go for your favorite scent first.

1. Make sure that you have all the supplies that you need. Unless you have really taken to making your own glycerin soap on a regular basis, you're likely going to have to do a little planning to purchase what you need to begin.
2. Prepare your soap molds before you begin melting your soap mixture.
3. Get all the ingredients you're going to add into your soap organized.

4. Melt the glycerin soap in a double boiler. By doing this you avoid the potential of the mixture being scorched to the bottom and allowing the soap to come to a boil.
5. Add in remaining ingredients and stir.
6. Pour the soap mixture into the molds, cleaning away any excess spills on the sides.
7. Spritz the molds with the rubbing alcohol (unless you are doing a clear soap).
8. Allow the soap to cool, which usually takes an hour or two. You'll just want to ensure that the soap is completely hardened in the mold.
9. Remove the soap from the mold. Or, if you just dried it in one large block so you could cut it, cut it into the bar sizes you want.
10. Congratulations to you! It's time to enjoy the soap you've created.

By following these basic steps you can make just about any soap you imagine. After a bit of time you'll grow more comfortable and confident in the entire process, which is when the real fun begins! And you're going to love it.

The Mint Connection

Most people really enjoy the smell of mint. Making a mint-based glycerin soap is a smart choice for anyone who is looking for something refreshing and different—plus bars of soap with mint infusions are very beautiful. So, consider these 4 recipes if you want to give yourself a treat or treat someone you like to a special gift that is handmade by you. Remember--- follow the instructions listed out in the previous chapter.

Mint Mania

Mint is a wonderful scent to have and this bar has proven to help those who have acne prone skin to find a healthy (and great smelling) solution to help them fight the bacteria that leads to acne. It's important to feel good about ourselves and this bar helps people do just that, while also giving them a blast of a great scent.

You will need:

- Glycerin soap base—one pound (use clear)
- Finely chopped mint leaves—enough to equal 1 tbsp.
- Peppermint Essential Oil—5 drops
- Spearmint Essential Oil—5 drops

Use this bar twice a day—in the morning and before bedtime—to improve the quality of your skin. Whether you get blemishes frequently or occasionally, and even not at all, you'll appreciate how this bar makes your skin feel.

Mint and Lavender Tranquility Bar

We don't like to exaggerate, but let us say—one of the best scents ever! You cannot go wrong with making this soap or using it. It's genuinely a joy and if nothing else, it will force you to pause and breathe in. Lessen your stress and get creative with this great soap.

The ingredients that you will need include:

- Clear glycerin soap base—8 ounces
- Lavender leaves—1 tsp crushed lavender leaves
- Fresh organic mint leaves—1 tsp crushed mint leaves
- Lavender Essential Oil—8 drops
- Spearmint Essential Oil—3 drops
- Eucalyptus Essential Oil—3 drops

As the mint and lavender begin to work their magic together, be prepared for the most tranquil, lift-you-up, soap making adventure of a lifetime.

Chocolate and Mint Divine

Is it a dessert? Is it a drink? No! It's a bar of soap that is like a calorie free dessert for your hands. This soap is fun and beautiful. Most of the people who really love this soap have said that it is the perfect festive accent to have around during the holidays for entertainment times, or for blissful gifts for those you want to show gratitude towards.

Use it however you like, just get these ingredients to make it happen:

- Glycerin soap—1 pound of clear soap
- Mint leaves—1/2 cup of crushed leaves (fresh or dried)
- Cocoa powder—1 tbsp. of cocoa powder (for coloring—if you want a richer color use a little more)
- Peppermint Essential Oil—20 drops

- Chocolate Essential Oil (or concentrate)—10 drops

These bars are fantastic because they are easy to make, despite looking very beautiful and complex. You're really going to enjoy this one!

Mint Love

If you can't get enough mint, you won't be able to get enough of this fantastic bar. It smells so great, but the scent it leaves on your skin is very subtle. Imagine walking along and getting a sudden surprise by a burst of fragrance from wild mind. It's that type of awesome. You can be the world's wild mint plant—or, just your own. Your call!

To get going with your Mint Love project, you will need:

- Clear glycerin soap—4 ounces
- Crushed and chopped fresh mint leaves—1 tsp
- Eucalyptus Essential Oil—1 drop
- Spearmint Essential Oil—1 drop
- Peppermint Essential Oil—1 drop
- Vitamin E capsule—1 capsule's contents

Are you feeling the love for mint yet? We're sure hoping that we happen to walk by you after you make and use this bar. It's absolutely fantastic!

Rolling
With The Rosemary

The herbal woodsy scent of rosemary makes it an excellent herb for cooking, as well all know, but also for creating glycerin soaps. Women are drawn to it and it's a soap that is appealing to men, as well. We're really excited to get your thoughts on these 4 recipes. Remember—follow the instructions listed out in the previous chapter.

The Rosemary Rage

Rosemary—nature's great exfoliation herb: only not everybody knows that, but now you do and it's your chance to create a bar that will invigorate your senses while it exfoliates your skin.

You will need:

- Clear glycerin soap—4 ounces
- Ground and dried rosemary leaves—1/4 cup (it's important to make them as fine as possible)
- Rosemary Essential Oil—12 drops

With exfoliating soap, it is important to not be too harsh with it or to use it too much, as you can overdo it. With this fantastic bar, it's recommended to do a gentle exfoliation every other day, just after you get out of the shower.

Rosemary and Lavender Love

A soap with a unique look that is beautiful and festive, as well as highly functional and great to actually use. Yes, we admit that some of these soaps are so beautiful that everyone is hesitant to be the first one to use them. Prepare for it and get over it, because you don't want to deny yourself this soap (or any of the soaps) awesome ability to clean your hands, clean your body, and make you feel great about your natural pursuits to better health through every day household products. Let's get creative!

You'll need:

- Clear glycerin soap—4 ounces
- Fresh rosemary leaves—chopped leaves from 3 sprigs (about 1 tbsp.)
- Fresh lavender leaves—1 tsp of crushed leaves
- Lavender Essential Oil—6 drops

- Rosemary Essential Oil—3 drops

This is a calming and soothing scent, which makes it wonderful for use on even the smallest of hands. In addition, a small bar of this near where you go to sleep can actually help your senses calm your mind so you can drift off to a blissful place of rest. Soap is a wonderful way to bring safe aromatherapy methods into the household that can't burn little hands (like a candle diffuser might).

It's Thyme for Rosemary Glycerin Soap Bar

Caution: making this bar smells so good you might feel like you're sitting in an Italian kitchen. But it can be your kitchen! The earthy, woodsy scents of this bar really are fantastic and even the "toughest" guys on the block will take a secret indulgence in this bar.

To make this fantastic bar you will need:

- Glycerin soap—5 ounces of clear

- Tea Tree Essential Oil—6 drops

- Rosemary leaves—1 tsp of fresh, chopped leaves

- Thyme—1 tsp of leaves (freshly plugged from the twig)

- Rosemary Essential Oil—2 drops

Think about the great ways that you can bring a little bit of a home cooking feel to your home by making soaps like these. They are appealing, their scent is not overpowering—it's inviting—and they are beautiful, too!

Rugged Rosemary Renegade

Out of all the glycerin soap bars out there, this one is amazing for men. They love the scent and women love the scent on them. It's rugged and appealing, and a whole slew of other good sensations rolled into one! Want to give a gift that will surprise someone more than make them wonder if it's a hint—give this one. Just one scent, that's all it took!

The ingredients for this renegade bar are:

- Glycerin soap base—4 ounces of clear
- Chopped fresh rosemary leaves—1 tbsp.
- Rosemary Essential Oil—1 drop
- Musk Essential Oil—1 drop

Have fun making this bar. As you can tell, it's also very easy to make (as all the recipes you've read are), and this one is definitely worth it! It smells so good—and not just to the guys, but to everyone! Think of those scents like the smell of your grandpa's pipe from long ago. They created a memory. This bar is one for memories in the making!

Fruity-Tooty and Fabulous

Fruit scents are ones that many people just naturally love. They make us happy and are fantastic to inhale, bringing about energy at times or a sense of tranquility and harmony at other times. Having access to glycerin soaps with these scents is wonderful for your senses, as well as great for your skin's health. With these 4 recipes you're going to be ready to indulge yourself in a fruity-tooty and fabulous way. Remember—follow the instructions listed out in the previous chapter.

Orange You Going to X-presso Yourself!

A wonderful and unique soap blend, this soap has such an invigorating and unique scent that you'll enjoy just smelling it when you enter into a room. Or perhaps you'll be inspired to go enjoy the company of friends at your favorite coffee house. It truly creates an experience to remember.

To make this fantastic bar, you'll need:

- Glycerin soap base—1 pound of either clear or white
- Organic cocoa butter—3 tbsp.
- Organic coconut oil—1 tbsp. (a wonderful ingredient to use for cooking and many other things, as well)
- Finely ground free trade coffee—1/4 cup
- Orange Essential Oil—10 drops
- Coffee Essential Oil (or equivalent of a concentrate)—5 drops

This bar is wonderful to make from beginning to end. As you go through the process, don't forget to make yourself a cup of coffee to enjoy with the journey. After all, through glycerin soap you are definitely beginning to x-presso yourself!

Strawberry Heaven

The scent of strawberries reminds us of some of the most wonderful memories we may have with food, fun, and wonderful weather. That is why this bar of soap is just like a bit of heaven, ideal for washing your hands and enjoying a waft of strawberries as you go about your day. Caution—may make you hungry to eat strawberries frequently!

You will need:

- Glycerin soap base—5 ounces (both pink and red really make this bar look beautiful)
- Poppy seeds—1/8 tsp
- Strawberries—1/4 cup of pureed strawberries
- Strawberry Fragrance Oil—10 drops

It will be easy to enjoy this fantastic soap, as it works as great as it smells. Just be cautious if you are allergic to strawberries, as that will mean that this is not the soap for you.

Lemon Lime Divine

Whether you are looking to infuse your skin with some wonderful nutrients or just give yourself a blast of summer-time feeling energy in the middle of the winter, you'll love this bar for its looks and its function.

To make this you will need:

- Glycerin soap base—4 ounces of clear (it's very important to use the clear base, as it looks the best. If you need a second choice, go with white).
- Lemon peel—1 tbsp. grated
- Lime peel—1 tbsp. grated
- Organic extra virgin olive oil—1 tbsp.
- Lemon Essential Oil—3 drops
- Lime Essential Oil—3 drops

This bar can go into many shapes, but most people have commented that it has such a beautiful and unique appearance that they prefer the rectangular or square bars for it (larger or smaller sizes).

The Facial Fruit Smoothie

Give your skin the gift of a smoothie by enjoying this amazing bath bar. Its light and refreshing scent is as amazing as is its ability to make your skin feel great. You cannot go wrong with healthier, glowing, and great smelling skin.

To make this great glycerin soap you will need:

- Glycerin soap—1 pound
- Raspberries—2 tbsp. pureed
- Blueberries—2 tbsp. pureed
- Goat milk—2 tbsp. (powdered, if at all possible; otherwise powdered 2% milk will work as a substitute)
- Coconut oil—1 tsp.
- Shea butter—1 tsp.

This is a fantastic bar to use on a daily basis, and for anything. It's great for washing hands, taking baths, and your shower routine, as well.

Tea Glee

Tea is nourishing for the soul and fantastic for the body—both inside and out. This is why daily use of tea based glycerin soaps is good for you and is an extra little step that you can take to keep everyone healthier, often without them even realizing it. Show the people you love that the little things do count toward the big picture with some tea-based glycerin soaps. These 4 will be a great way to get you started! Remember—follow the instructions listed out in the previous chapter.

Roses and Tea Bar

The benefits and delightful scent of this bar are fantastic and exquisite to be around. As you make it, your living area will come alive with a calming scent that is ideal for bringing out the tranquil within your spirit when it's needed most. Or maybe you are ready to indulge in a little pampering bath session.

To bring on this lovely tea and roses moment in your life you will need:

- Glycerin soap base (clear or pink)—4 ounces
- Rose Essential Oil—12 drops
- Tea Tree Essential Oil—6 drops
- Jojoba oil—1/2 tsp
- Rose buds—1/4 cup of dried and grounded rose buds

This is a great bar for making two smaller bars with (ornate) or else one larger bar—your call.

Many people have liked the thought of two smaller bars, because it is such a lovely fragrance that sustains in a mild and inviting manner!

Chamomile Comfort

This is a beautiful bar of soap with minimal fragrance, but wonderful properties. Chamomile is known for calming the heart and soothing the soul, as well as relaxation, in general. It's amazing how a gesture as seemingly "mindless" as washing your hands with a soap like this and taking note of its subtle fragrance can help change your perspective in an instant.

To make the glycerin soap that provides comfort you will need:

- Glycerin soap base—4 ounces of the clear soap (can use white if preferred)
- Chamomile tea leaves—1 tbsp. of loose tea leaves (organic)
- Tea Tree Essential Oil—3 drops
- Chamomile Essential Oil—3 drops
- Lemon Essential Oil—1 drop

This is an ideal soap for all uses, and a wonderful way to help restore the sanity in your crazy, hectic life. Just breathe in and say, "Ah"!

The Tea Tree Experience

A great soap for all occasions and one that is appealing and refreshing to everyone's senses. This nourishing and neutralizing soap is great for individuals who have combination skin (dry in some areas and oily in others), as well as a great bar soap to use for shaving your legs. And, as always, you can just clean your hands with it, too. Does it do everything? Well, not quite. It doesn't make itself; that's where you come in.

Here is what you need to make The Tea Tree Experience:

- Glycerin soap base—9 ounces
- Tea Tree Essential Oil—12 drops
- Loose leaf organic white (or green) tea—1 tbsp.
- Rosemary Essential Oil—1 drop

Begin to indulge yourself—now! This soap smells as wonderful as it makes you feel. And are you worth it? Absolutely!

Tea Time 2 Bath Time

Two wonderful things that we associate with calming down and pampering ourselves are tea time and bath time. Never the ones to sit idly by and not try new things, we came up with this awesome glycerin soap recipe that goes just a bit crazy with your calming efforts by combining both things into one. Brilliant, yes? Let's get you creating this brilliant recipe.

You will need:

- Clear glycerin soap—4 ounces
- Lavender leaves—1 tsp crushed
- Green tea leaves—1 tsp crushed
- Lemon Essential Oil—2 drops
- Lavender Essential Oil—3 drops
- Tea Tree Essential Oil—3 drops

Please follow the instructions outlined in the previous chapter. Then you wait and relax your mind to the thought of having your tea time in the bath—simply wonderful!

Oatmeal
Obsessions

The benefits of oatmeal are numerous. For our insides, a diet with oatmeal included is good for cholesterol management; receiving a satisfying meal that will give you the energy you need to navigate your day, and, in general, it tastes pretty good—either plain or with a few of your favorite toppings on it. When it comes to beauty products for external use, oatmeal is equally wonderful. Glycerin soaps with oatmeal in them are ideal for exfoliating the skin while nourishing it at the same time. They are gentle, and they leave your skin feeling soft and wonderful. After you experiment with these 4 recipes, you're going to love having an oatmeal obsession. Remember—follow the instructions listed out in the previous chapter.

Oatmeal and Blueberry Bar

This soap is beautiful and a great one to put into shaped soap molds if you're set to go big. The results are wonderful and fantastic, and we've especially enjoyed seeing people put this particular soap in the molds that have water themes to them (example: seashells).

You will need:

- Melt and pour glycerin soap base—4 ounces
- Ground dried oats—1/3 cup
- Blueberries—1/4 cup of pureed blueberries
- Blueberry Essential Oil (or fragrant oil if you cannot find)—14 drops

The color and texture of this particular glycerin soap is so beautiful—one of our favorites. Many people have also substituted raspberries and strawberries for the blueberry ingredients, as well. It's your call, but it's a call worth making. Soaps like this are wonderful for decoration and also beneficial for pampering and washing yourself in a nice, warm bath.

Oatmeal, Honey, and Vanilla Beauty Blast Bar

If glycerin soap could ever be a healthy desert, it would be in the form of this bar. It smells so good and is so good for your skin. On a fairly consistent basis, people comment how this bar is the favorite of everyone in their house—young, old, male, and female!

To make this you will need:

- Glycerin soap—2 pounds of clear soap
- Honey—1/8 cup (remember to have it slightly warmed or at least at room temperature)
- Oatmeal—3/4 cup of ground oatmeal
- Vitamin E oil—1 tsp (you can substitute 1 tsp of sunflower oil, as well)
- Vanilla Essential Oil—12 drops

You're going to get a lot of bars out of this batch and it will last a long time (store in an airtight container). If you have special occasions and holidays coming up, this is also an ideal bar to give as part of small gifts of gratitude and for thoughtful gestures, as well.

Peach and Oatmeal Exfoliating Bar

Lightly scented and refreshing, this fantastic bar is like an exfoliating dream. Its scent is nice and the way it leaves your skin feeling is blissful. We've found it to also be wonderful for the elbows and knees in helping smooth them out and prevent those little bumps that occasionally find their way there. You'll be feeling peachy about this one.

To make it you will need:

- Glycerin soap base—4 ounces of clear soap
- 1 medium organic peach—pureed (1/4 cup)
- Oatmeal—1 tbsp.
- Jojoba oil—1/8 tsp

When you are ready to use this bar, be prepared to walk away from the experience with a smile on your face and knowing that you've just done a wonderful thing for your skin. For elbows and knees, you can use this daily, but for your face, go every other day. And remember—always be gentle!

The Avocado Oatmeal Adventure

Avocados are not only a super food, they are also a super ingredient for glycerin soap giving you the opportunity to pamper your skin the way you try to pamper the rest of your body by a healthier diet. This is a nourishing glycerin soap bar that is sure to leave you feeling replenished and smiling. Ready to get going?

You will need:

- Glycerin soap base—4 ounces of clear soap
- Avocado—you'll only need ½ of it, make sure it's baked and pureed
- Tea Tree Essential Oil—2 drops
- Vitamin E—1 small capsule, squeezed

This is a fantastic bar of soap that will last you awhile, but make sure that you have another one on reserve, because a day without it might feel like you've just taken a step backwards in your soft, supple skin pursuit!

Divinely Different
In a World All Their Own

People who love to make glycerin soaps eventually love to experiment, too. They may be out and about somewhere and a wonderful combination of scents invades their senses, creating the highly appealing thought of how great it would be to capture those scents in a soap. Or maybe you have a special need you are trying to tend to, whether it's as part of your external or internal beauty and health plan, and you can create a soap that helps remind you of what you want to achieve. All inspiring and great ideas, are definitely ones worth experimenting with. The 6 recipes we're sharing with you in this section are definitely experiments gone right! Remember—follow the instructions listed out in the previous chapter.

Ah, What a Relief Bar!

This excellent bar is ideal for people who are experiencing skin irritations, whether they are from too much sun or from hives or allergic reactions. This combination of ingredients is gentle and smoothing, making it an excellent choice. Using this type of gentle bar on smaller children is also a smart move, as their skin is often very delicate.

You will need:

- 4 ounces of glycerin soap base (an earthy green color is great for this bar)
- Aloe Vera gel—1/8 cup (remember to scrape the cup good when you are creating)
- Nettle leaf powder—2 tbsp.

Follow the instructions that are listed out at the beginning of the recipe section and in a few hours, you'll be able to begin feeling the relief on your skin. NOTE: do not use the rubbing alcohol spritzer with this recipe.

Chocolate and Cinnamon Swirl Bar

This is a beautiful and unique bar of soap, ideal for gifts, accents to your home, and also to use, of course! Don't be shy. The one thing that you will find different with this recipe than most others is that you will divide your melted soap in half. That's how you make the swirls. But don't worry, it's as simple as mixing a marble cake together!

You will need:

- Glycerin soap base—1 pound (either beige or white recommended)

- Cocoa butter—1 tbsp.

- Divide this melted mixture in half. In one of those halves, you will need:

- Ground organic cinnamon—1/4 tsp

- Chocolate Essential Oil—12 drops

- Cocoa powder—1 tbsp. for color (use a bit more if you want it to be a richer brown color)

Then you will swirl these two colors together, creating the distinction between them and pour them into your molds. Follow the rest of your basic steps and you'll be set to enjoy this beautiful and amazing bar of glycerin soap.

Aloe Vera Gel and Cucumber Peel Rejuvenator

With a refreshing and rejuvenating sensation to it, everyone will love how great they feel after using this glycerin soap on any part of their body. The ingredients in it are almost magical when working together to work against unwanted wear, tear, and even damage on your skin. They say that age is a state of mind and after using this bar, your state of mind may very well tell you that you're younger than you've ever been!

To make this single batch serving you need:

- Glycerin soap base—3 ounces of clear brand
- 1 small organic cucumber—1/4 cup of grated cucumber—fresh
- Aloe Vera gel—1 tbsp.
- Cucumber Essential Oils (or something comparable for glycerin soaps)—12 drops

Using this bar is a wonderful experience, one that you will love and others in your household may love, too. Once you see how popular it is, it's a good idea to make another one right away, as you won't want to run out of this great bar!

Sunshine in a Bar

There are so many good things in this gentle, multi-purpose glycerin bar that we can't possibly put it into one category. So let's just think of it as a bright sun with rays of benefits flying out from it in every direction. Quite the visual, isn't it? Well, it's a perfect one to take with you as you begin making this bar.

The ingredients that you will need include:

- Glycerin soap—8 ounces of clear
- Lemon Essential Oil—2 drops
- Orange Essential Oil—2 drops
- Tea Tree Essential Oil—2 drops
- Chamomile tea—1/2 tsp of loose dry tea
- Orange zest—1 tsp (from an organic orange, of course)
- Jojoba oil—1 tsp

This fantastic recipe makes two bars so you'll have an excellent chance to spread the sunshine to someone else, or be selfish and keep it all to yourself! Your call. If you happen to find a sunshine shaped soap mold, you definitely will want to give that a try. It makes for a beautiful bar with rays of hope blasting out in every direction.

The Fiesta

Let's start off by saying—this is not a bar of soap that you will want to use, as the ingredients aren't gentle. This one is simply for decorations and giving people festive gifts that are unique and awesome. But it is fun to make, and actually can make for a fun project with kids, too!

You will need:

- Glycerin soap base—8 ounces of clear base
- Peppers—6 small tiny string bean style peppers of all colors (each one cut in half)
- Cilantro—1 tbsp. of chopped fresh cilantro

Yes, it sounds crazy, but it really is fun to experiment with glycerin soaps with whatever ingredients you feel compelled to experiment with. This particular innovation came from a lady who was holding a Mexican fiesta party for her mother-in-law, who was visiting in the States. The effort was noted, and it was definitely a unique decoration!

Flower Power Bar

This bar is really fun to create and a great way to use up those flowers in your gardens before they go bad at the end of their season. Regardless of what flowers they are. We'll show you one variation that some people have done and raved about, as it offers a beautiful display and the nutrients in flower pedals are actually good for the skin, as well. And if you're someone who's been unfortunate enough to find out you're allergic to flowers, this bar will let you enjoy them without the bouts of sneezing that used to follow!

To make this bar, you will need:

- Glycerin soap—8 ounces of clear soap
- Rose pedals—1 tsp dried and crushed
- Marigold pedals—1 tsp dried and crushed
- Tulips—1 tsp dried and crushed
- Black-eyed Susans—1 tsp of the pedals dried and crushed

- Any preserved stamens that you like as an ornate piece for center of bar (optional, of course)
- Jojoba oil—1 tsp

What we really love about this bar is you can take the time to collect and dry the pedals throughout the year and make a batch once a year. Maybe even in the dead of winter when you're longing for flowers (if you're not fortunate to live in a place where flowers are in bloom all year long). This one is a great gift to give for showers, friends, and the gardening enthusiast, as well. Very clever. What flowers do you have access to so you can make your very own Flower Power Bar?

Conclusion

Most people have a natural tendency to associate scents with memories, which makes scents more powerful than we often realize in our conscious minds. Likewise, many people associate what they make themselves with love. Furthermore, they're going to use ingredients that are good for them—and good for others. With taking the initiative to make your own glycerin soap you are doing so much good, while also having so much fun. This is not just "good", it's great. Don't you love the thought of your kids someday saying, "Mom [or Dad], I used to love the smell of that soap you made so much. I'd sneak into the bathroom and smell it all the time." Sounds crazy, but testimonials such as that have stemmed from endeavors such as the one we've shared with you.

Hopefully you're inspired to give glycerin soap making a try. We've laid everything out for you, giving you the basic information and the specific steps to take, hoping you'll be inspired to act. But in the end, only you can take the steps forward. Most people who begin the process of making these soaps find a wonderful skill is awaiting them that is good for their creative selves, relaxing selves, and quite literally, their physical selves, too! Do you want those things for you? If you do, then you definitely want to try some of these recipes out!

Printed in Great Britain
by Amazon